UNTAMED ENCOUNTERS

UNTAMED ENCOUNTERS

CONTEMPORARY JEWELRY FROM EXTRAORDINARY GEMSTONES

MIMI LIPTON

With 260 colour illustrations

Thames & Hudson

First published in the United Kingdom in 2014 by
Thames & Hudson Ltd, 181A High Holborn, London WC1V 7QX

www.thamesandhudson.com

First published in 2014 in hardcover in the United States of America by
Thames & Hudson Inc., 500 Fifth Avenue, New York, New York 10110

thamesandhudsonusa.com

Untamed Encounters: Contemporary Jewelry from Extraordinary Gemstones
© 2014 Mimi Lipton

Photography: Noelle Hoeppe
Design: Malgosia Szemberg
Introduction: Narisa Chakrabongse

British Library Cataloguing-in-Publication Data
A catalogue record for this book is available from the British Library

Library of Congress Catalog Card Number 2014932769

ISBN 978-0-500-97063-8

Printed and bound in China by C & C Offset Printing Co. Ltd

CONTENTS

INTRODUCTION

NARISA CHAKRABONGSE

'Something rich and strange'

Ariel in Shakespeare's *The Tempest*

A slight figure wanders along a semi-deserted, sandy beach in Khao Lak, southern Thailand. Despite the beauty of the shimmering sea, her eyes concentrate only on the raised beach of pebbles, shells and bleached coral. Suddenly she stoops and picks up a lump of coral, its creamy skin pitted with delicate lacy indentations like the surface of the moon.

A few months later, the coral oval lies on a dramatic glass table in a London flat, embellished by a thin circle of 22 carat gold and small semi-precious pink stones (p. 167). Together with a matching bleached coral ring (p. 166), it is surrounded by a cornucopia of more than eighty equally unusual and dramatic pieces of jewelry. The low light at the back of the long, large room creates the impression of a dragon's hoard, a feeling heightened by the uncut stones glistening in their gold settings.

An emerald crystal hangs like a glowing green stalactite (p. 154); an undulating bangle in austere colours suggests tree rings or a pattern by Missoni (p. 65); a fiery blue Ethiopian opal gleams like an eye trapped in the coils of a dark snake (p. 74); a delicate pearl abacus complements a carefully carved, deep orange amber roundel (p. 81); from the same material but very different in feeling is a necklace of white Baltic amber and asymmetric gold hoops (p. 59), the graceful patterns in the amber like the mountains on a Chinese scroll.

So diverse and original are these pieces of jewelry, more akin to miniature sculptures than the traditional and predictable products of many famous makers, that it is difficult to comprehend that they have been created over the space of only six years by the vision and flair of Mimi Lipton and her collaborators – Ram Rijal, Daniel Azaro, Nan Nan Liu, Ornella Iannuzzi, Disa Allsopp, Helga Mogensen and Syann van Niftrik.

In truth, the path that has led to these creations has been long. It seems as if the urge to create jewelry has been gestating in Mimi's mind for decades. Talking about her work, Mimi is somewhat diffident and amazed when she sees all the pieces laid out en masse. 'I feel like I have been sleepwalking for half my life,' she says, but 'creative dreaming' seems a more appropriate term than 'sleepwalking'. When pushed, she concedes: 'I did not know I was creative until recently as I received little encouragement when I was young. I do believe I have a very good eye, instinct and unusual taste.' It is the journey of Mimi's life that has brought her to this point, the jewelry forming a tapestry interwoven with all the places she has been, the exhibitions she has seen, the artists she has encountered, the clothes she has worn, and the students she has met at college degree shows and art fairs.

Mimi was born in Vienna and lived in Austria until the Anschluss of 1938 forced the family to flee their home and find a safe haven in England. In the early 1930s, Vienna still retained its atmosphere of culture and experiment in the arts and, although Mimi was too young to be consciously influenced, her father did take her to museums every Sunday, these precious interludes the only time they got to spend together. As with many children, the Egyptian section with its mummies made the greatest impression, together with a brilliantly coloured feathered cape from Brazil.

Her school years and early adulthood in Leeds soon gave way to a life in London during the Swinging Sixties, where she worked at the ICA as assistant curator to writer and critic Jasia Reichardt on a show entitled 'Cybernetic Serendipity'. At that time the ICA was a real centre for new ideas in London, seeing the launch of Pop Art, Op Art and Brutalist architecture. As her husband, Hansjörg Mayer, remarked recently: 'When you went to an opening at the ICA, you knew you would run into everyone in the London art world.'

Such an environment must have been extremely stimulating and exciting for someone like Mimi, who always was and has remained alive to new ideas and trends. There she met and became friends with many contemporary artists, such as John Latham and Bridget Riley, and most importantly Hansjörg Mayer, who was to become her lifelong partner and later her husband. Through Mayer, Mimi met other artists such as Richard Hamilton and Dieter Roth, and later became a dealer for Roth, Latham, Tom Phillips, Mark Boyle, Arnulf Rainer, André Thomkins and Franz Eggenschwiler. Perhaps it was from such artists that Mimi unconsciously assimilated the idea of using found objects in her work and the importance of retaining an integrity towards materials.

Apart from mixing in the art world, it was with Mayer that Mimi began a series of foreign travels to destinations throughout Europe, Africa and Asia, to places that were little visited at the time and not the tourist hotspots of today. Gradually she started acquiring important pieces of indigenous jewelry on these journeys. At first, these were mainly in silver, as in the magnificent Turkoman bracelets inset with carnelians or the hill tribe jewelry of the Golden Triangle in northern Thailand and Burma. Old ivory also featured in her collections – bracelets and Dinka rings, with some of the latter being transformed by Mimi in her jewelry. Studying and researching ethnic pieces in museum collections exposed Mimi to works of art from all over the world, and no doubt these enriching encounters with tribal arts allowed her to see and think about jewelry in quite different ways. They helped her to escape the constraints of the traditional and consider the extraordinary.

A trip to Tibet followed in 1985. It was long and arduous, but as a result Mimi became a lifelong supporter of Tibetan Buddhism and began an important collection of Tibetan *thangkas* and gold jewelry, which were described in the book *Gold Jewelry from Tibet and Nepal* by Jane Singer and subsequently toured as an exhibition at the Brunei Gallery in London in 1996–97, the Tropenmuseum in Amsterdam and elsewhere. It was soon after seeing the way in which Tibetan turquoise, coral and pearl were set off by their lush gold settings that Mimi decided to create her own jewelry in gold, this most precious, untarnishable metal that has served as a benchmark for objects of value since before history.

One of the defining and unusual characteristics of Mimi's work is the way that gemstones are allowed to remain just as they were formed in extreme conditions of immense heat and pressure millions of years ago. In addition, Mimi is not after purity of stone or clarity, but rather searches out beautiful colours and unusual formations. Thus, a ring by Ornella Iannuzzi features crystals of mossy green demantoid, a gemstone much favoured by Fabergé, set into an elaborately cast ring that echoes the crystalline structure of the stones (p. 49), or in a necklace by Ram Rijal, a smooth black coral torc is offset by crystal and aquamarines, both in their original natural state (p. 205).

In a similar fashion, freshwater pearls are prized for their unusual shapes (pp. 89, 147) and black coral is left to curve sinuously, its shapes echoed in gold (pp. 26–27), while red coral hangs proudly, its branches still intact (p. 183). Occasionally bleached coral and black are mixed and set together, as in the extraordinary brooch where a piece of white coral sits on a black branch like some strange lizard or praying mantis, its body encircled by gold and rubies, the head formed by a natural pearl (p. 96). The piece is paired with a bracelet of black coral, bleached coral and pearls (p. 133), appearing like some strange but beautiful sea creature, whose abstract shape was inspired by a Henry Moore. Another baroque pearl nestles in an exquisite fanlike setting (p. 115), its natural forms assuming almost sexual imagery.

If one strand in Mimi's collection is woven around respect for the material and the use of uncut stones, coral and pearls, another consists of transforming existing artefacts into something completely new and unexpected. These are often items that, when worn by the original owners, were signifiers of power and status.

In the early 1990s, while strolling in the back streets of Venice, Mimi came across small ovals of carved, deep orange amber. These intriguing, tactile objects are referred to by dealers as Liao ambers. The pieces found today are not from the period of that dynasty as the original Chinese amber was too brittle to survive. Instead they are carved from Baltic amber, found in the states bordering the Baltic Sea. As every school child knows, amber is fossilized tree resin and occurs in a range of hues, from white to deep orange, almost red. It has been highly valued as a gemstone since Neolithic times, and jewelry created from amber is found in many early cultures throughout the world. As well as having great beauty, amber is believed by many cultures to have healing properties. Such was the extent of the trade in this material that a so-called 'Amber Road' has even been posited. The early 18th-century copies of the Liao originals, worn as status symbols on the gowns of Chinese mandarins, are often delicately carved with birds and flowers. Her curiosity piqued, Mimi sought more and soon decided to create an individual collection. In the hands of three of Mimi's jewelry collaborators, Daniel, Ram and Helga, they have been transformed into eleven remarkable and diverse necklaces.

Six necklaces in this group have been designed by Daniel Azaro – each different and all very inventive. In one, a large carved amber forms the centrepiece of a gold torc, the tiny holes where it would once have been stitched onto a silk robe now filled in with gold (p. 164). In another, mirrors surrounded by vibrant blue kingfisher feathers, refined ornaments that originally would have adorned a Chinese fan, are interspersed with the rich, deep amber (p. 90), while in a third, the delicacy of freshwater pearls and a tiny abacus offset two roundels in umber-coloured amber (p. 81).

Daniel and Mimi have known each other for many years. Born in Buenos Aires and originally trained as an architect, he came to London in the early 1970s due to the political situation in Argentina, and became an inventive and skilful designer and jewelry maker.

Daniel speaks warmly of his work with Mimi and their friendship, which he clearly values: 'The enormous variety of work I've undertaken for Mimi over the years has made for a special partnership in terms of understanding each other's aesthetics. Each piece she commissions is like a riddle to be solved, and our long working relationship has given me an insight into how she envisages the piece being realized. Possibly we both bring out the best in each other, which is after all what collaboration strives for.

'Collaborating with Mimi is ever invigorating because of her forward approach and unrestricted views. Her noteworthy and unrelenting search for new places, and their cultures, has brought many rare objects into my hands and it has been a pleasure to transform these things into unique pieces of adornment. Her insatiable curiosity and desire to discover mean that she always brings intriguing materials to discuss, admire and ponder.'

The transformation of existing pieces of jewelry is also demonstrated in the ivory pieces, of which there are six. The agro-pastoral Dinka tribes inhabiting southern Sudan on both sides of the White Nile make jewelry from beads and ivory. Nineteenth-century Dinka pieces are pale and wonderfully smooth, the dark lines on some items enhancing the feeling of age. In Mimi's hands, rings are inset with small gemstones (p. 222) or worn as pendants accented by gold (p. 129); two ivory roundels from a headdress are combined with gold hoops whose forms create a chain of voids (p. 208), the shapes of which mimic the solid pieces, or the simple but powerful shapes of Dinka ivory rectangles are copied in gold (p. 69).

Mimi has not just used antique pieces as a starting point for her creations, but, ever alive to the possibilities of transformation, she has added gold and lapis lazuli to resin bangles by the contemporary Italian architect and designer Gaetano Pesce (p. 82). Interestingly, Pesce's path to jewelry making has been a similarly oblique one, as he began as an architect and has admitted that he also stumbled into jewelry making by accident.

Apart from always being on the lookout for interesting pieces to inspire her designs, Mimi is keen to bring on new talent and encourage young designers whom she discovers at degree shows and contemporary jewelry fairs. Such forays have resulted in the dramatic coiled torc in gold and oxidized silver by Disa Allsopp (p. 74) and the restrained yet beautiful and bold necklaces by a young Chinese designer, Nan Nan Liu. In the latter, the shapes of creamy white Baltic amber are echoed in irregular open hoops (p. 59), or two asymmetric tourmaline rectangles are picked up by the stark geometry of a gold chain (p. 38). Different again from the work of these two designers is a necklace using Liao amber, iron and driftwood by the Icelandic designer Helga Mogensen (p. 215). Here, the smooth roundness of the Liao ambers is offset by angular pieces of iron or gold and a small fragment of driftwood.

However, the jewelry maker with whom Mimi has collaborated the most is undoubtedly Ram Rijal. Born in Nepal with its centuries-old jewelry traditions, Ram trained as a goldsmith's apprentice with jewelry makers in Jaipur before branching out on his own. Based in Portobello Road in London, Ram first met Mimi when he sold her a couple of pieces of Tibetan gold jewelry and from that developed a friendship and a close working relationship. Ram says that he is half Hindu, half Buddhist, and his relaxed and laid-back demeanour is a perfect foil to Mimi's nervous energy and drive.

Mimi has said: 'When you take a stone or an existing antique piece to Ram and discuss how it should be, you never know exactly what you are going to get.' Nevertheless, the results speak for themselves and attest to an excellent working relationship that has produced extraordinary works of art. Over the years Ram has developed an instinctive understanding of what Mimi wants, and they share the same love of unusual stones and crystals. The first piece they created together is a strikingly rich combination of aquamarine, coral, amber, amethyst and gold beads (p. 143), and the range of jewelry has expanded to include both simple and intricate rings, bracelets and necklaces using a diverse range of precious and semi-precious stones from all over the world.

While Ram has sourced many of the raw materials himself, he acknowledges Mimi's uncanny talent for 'finding unusual and unique things and always knowing something is perfect as soon as she sees it'. Set in 22 carat gold, which has been intricately worked to create a distinctive finish, the one-off Ram–Mimi pieces are immediately identifiable.

The names of the stones in Mimi's jewelry evoke journeys to the far-flung corners of the world – Baltic amber, Tibetan corals, Madagascan demantoids, Burmese tourmalines, African ivories, Afghan lapis lazuli and Colombian emeralds, to name but a few. This rich hoard, fashioned by designers from France, Iceland, Barbados, Argentina, China, Nepal and South Africa, has the vision of Mimi Lipton as the common thread. The finished pieces reflect the life's journey, experience and truly seeing eye of a creative and multifaceted woman.

GALLERY

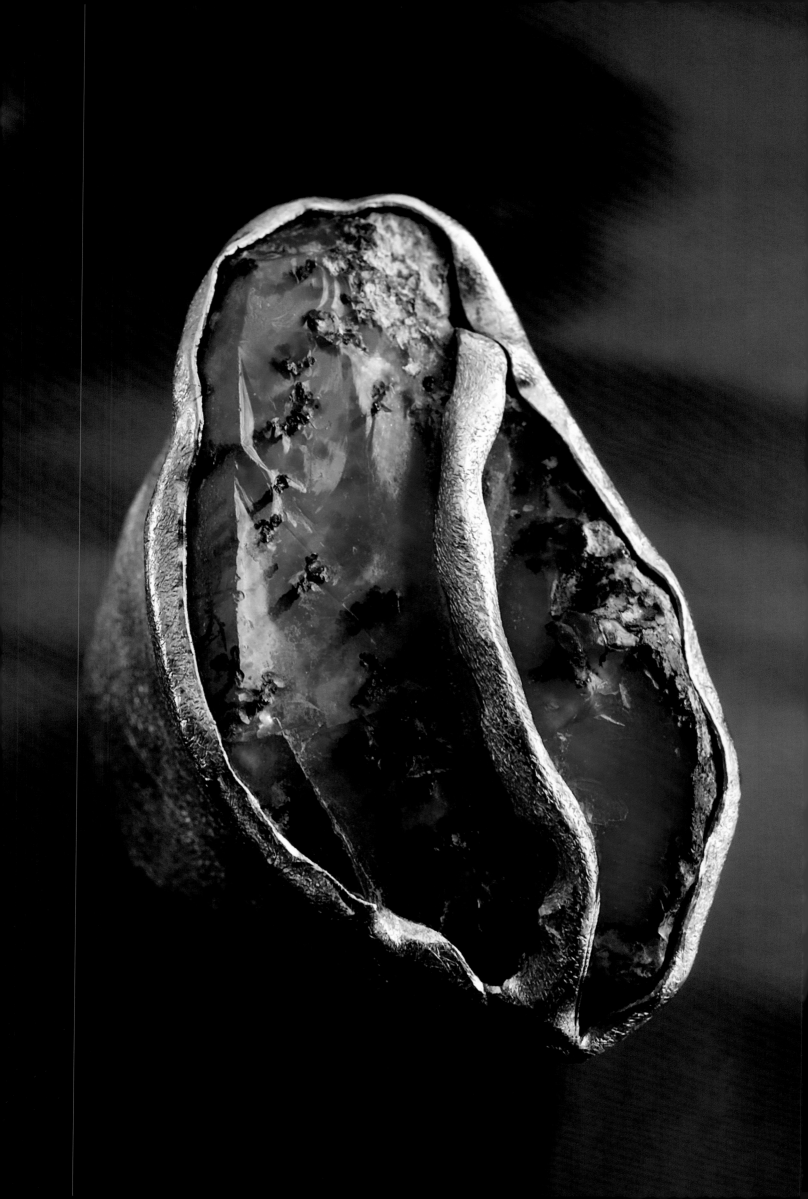

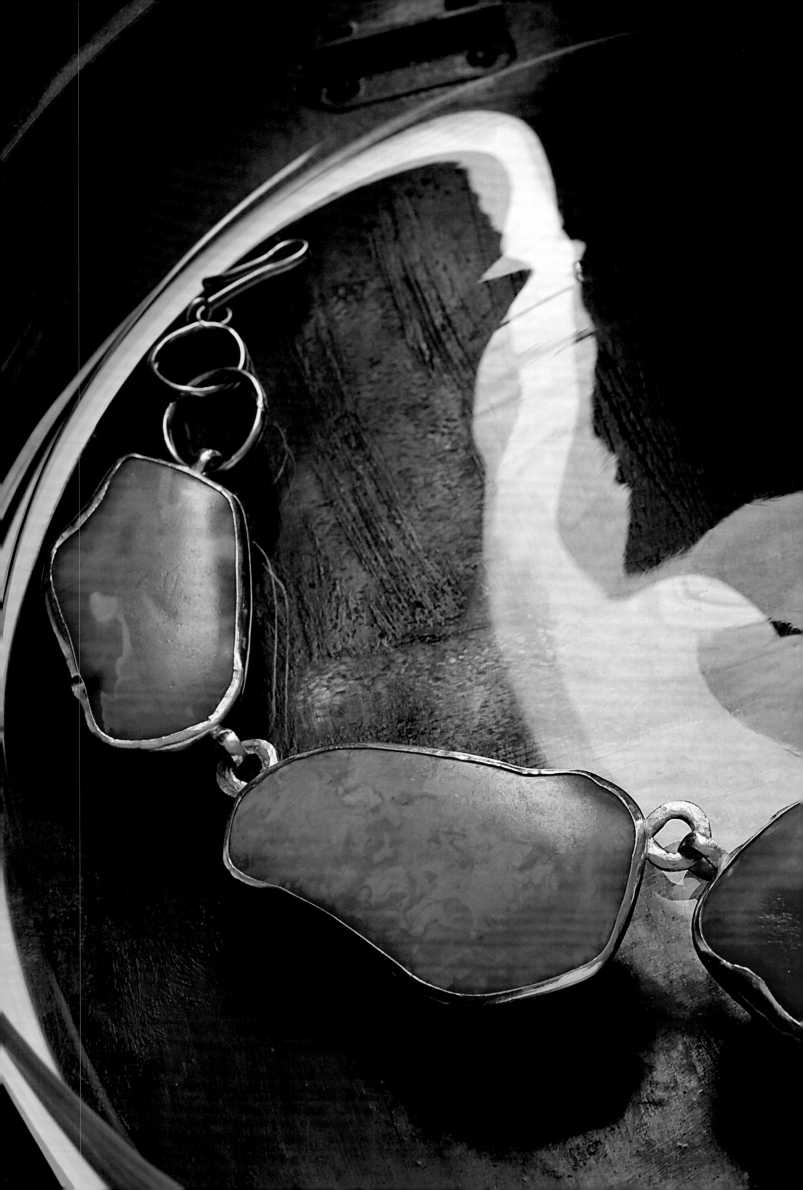

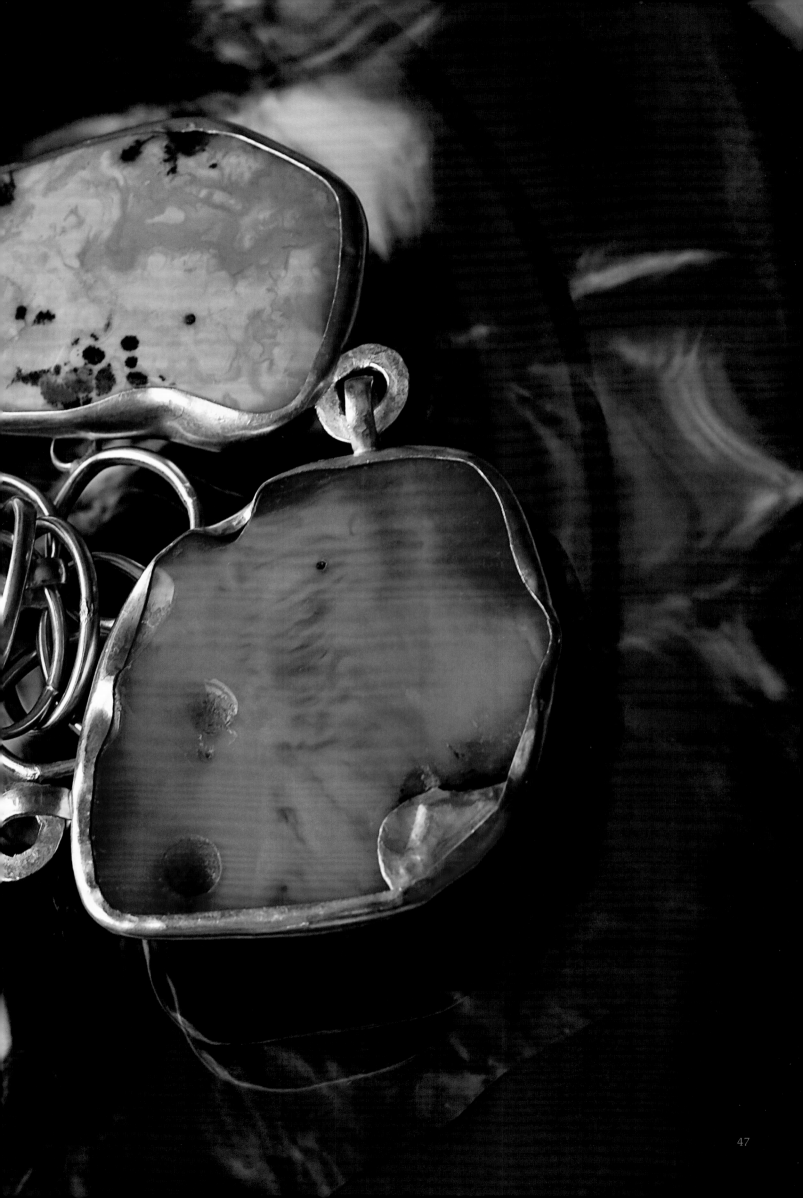

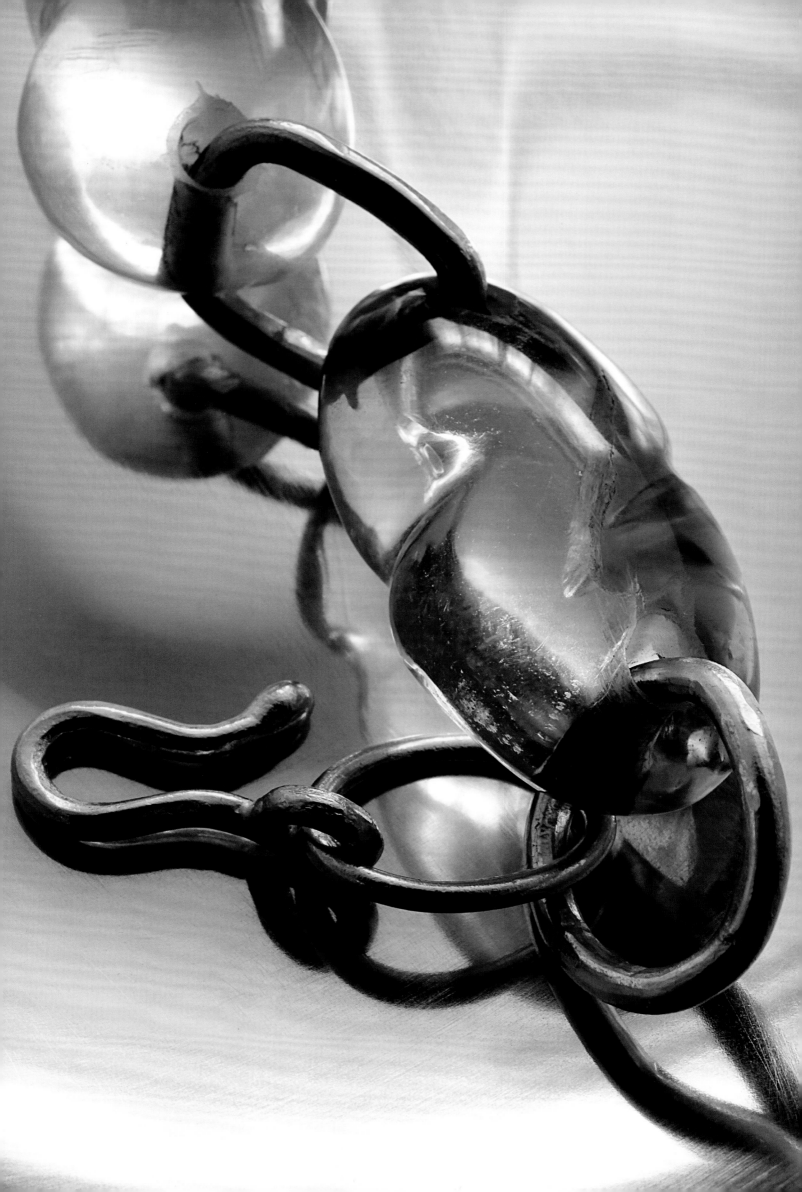

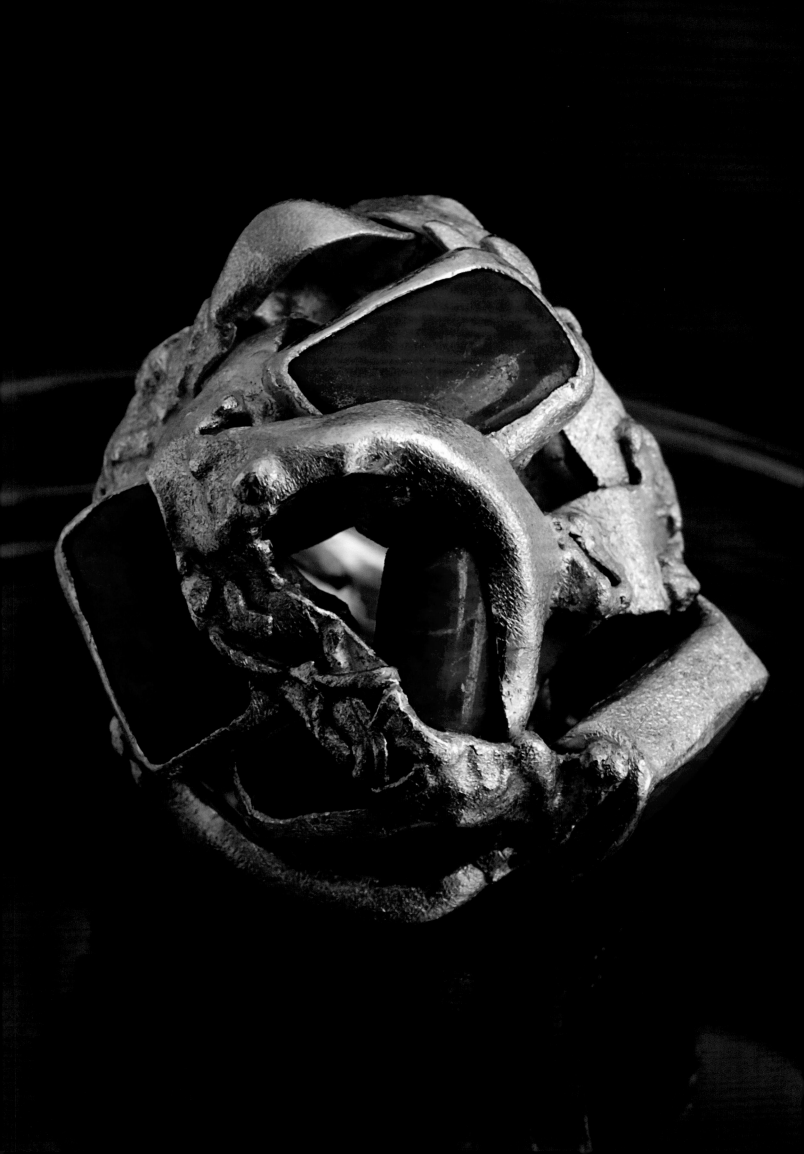

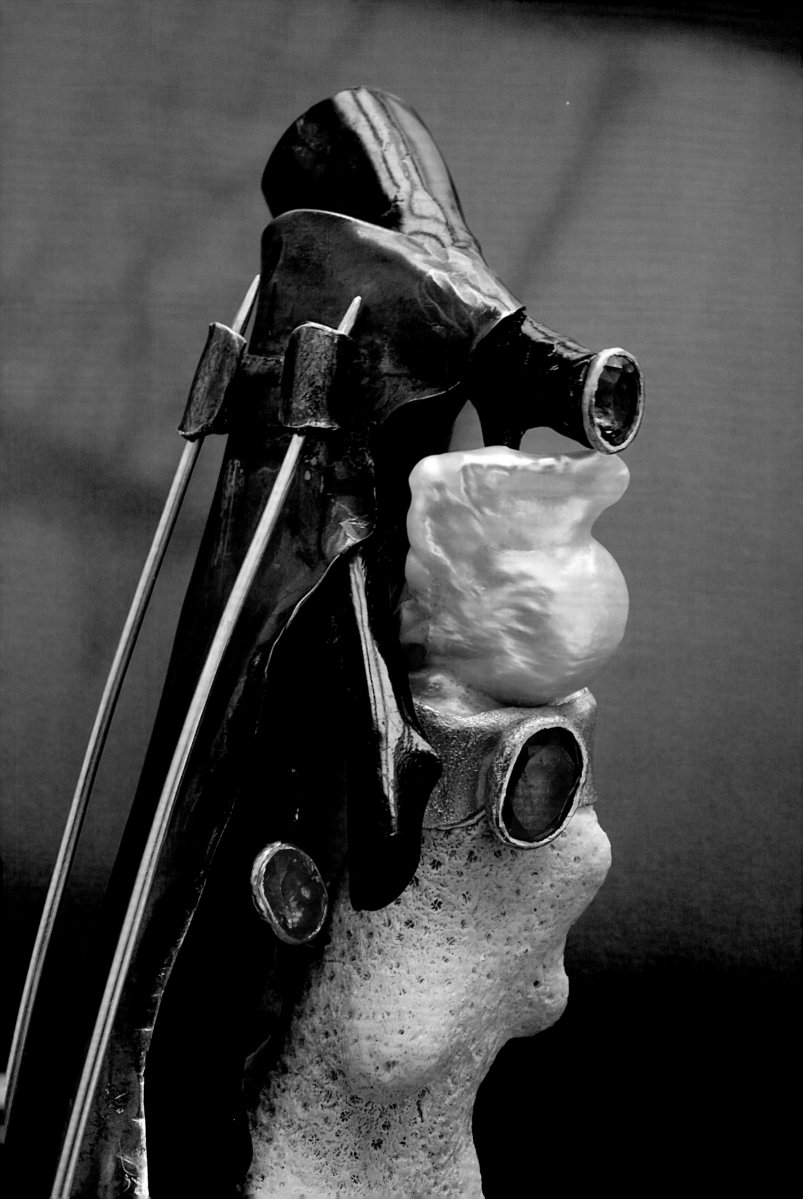

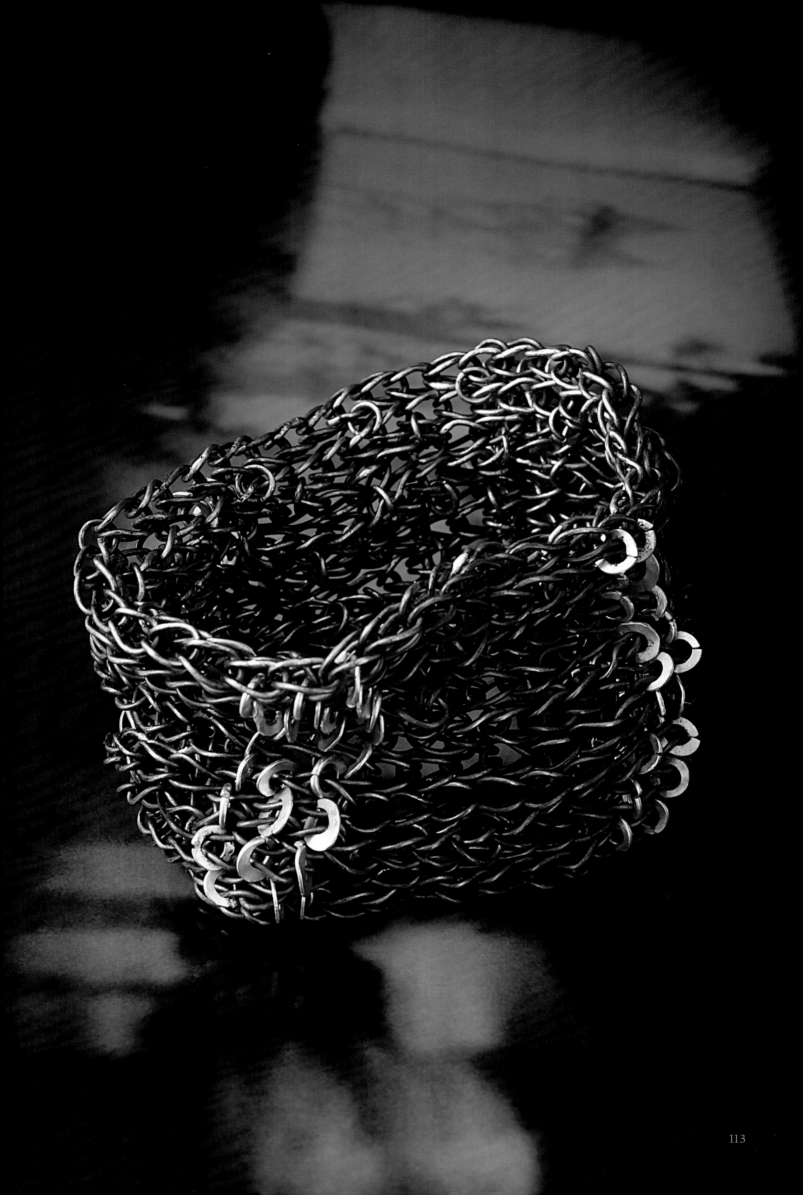

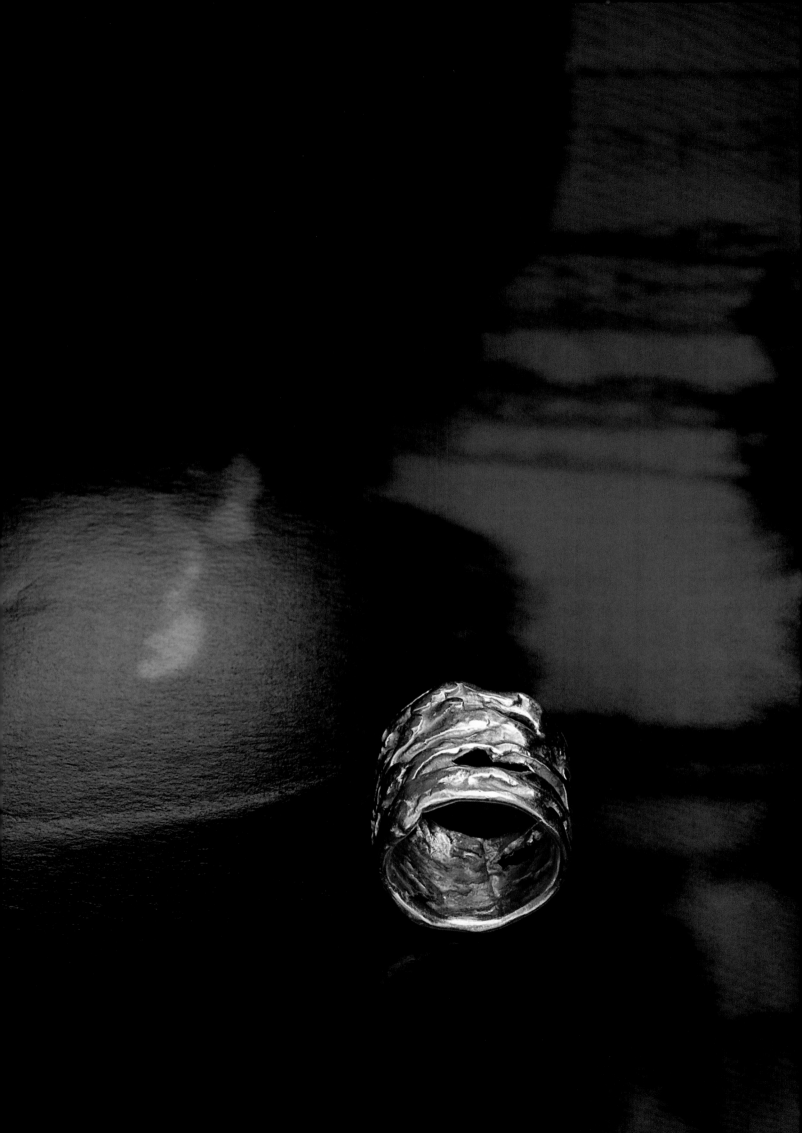

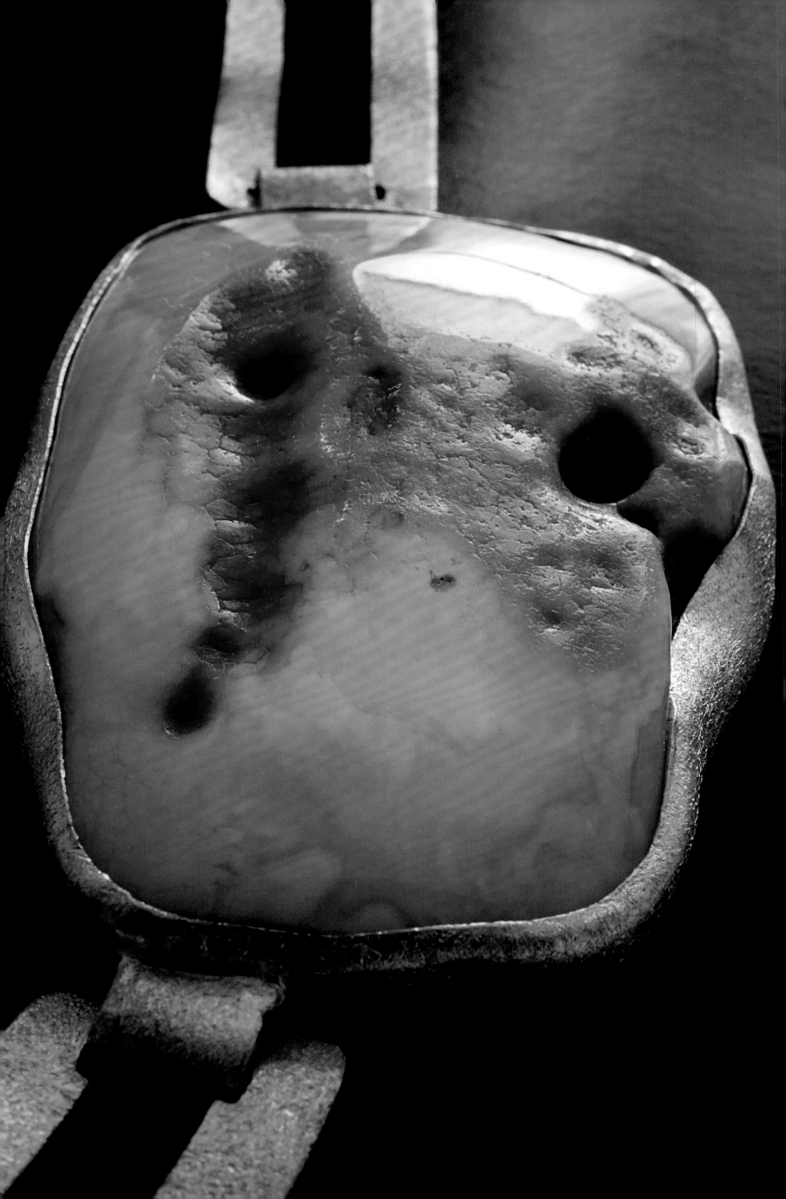

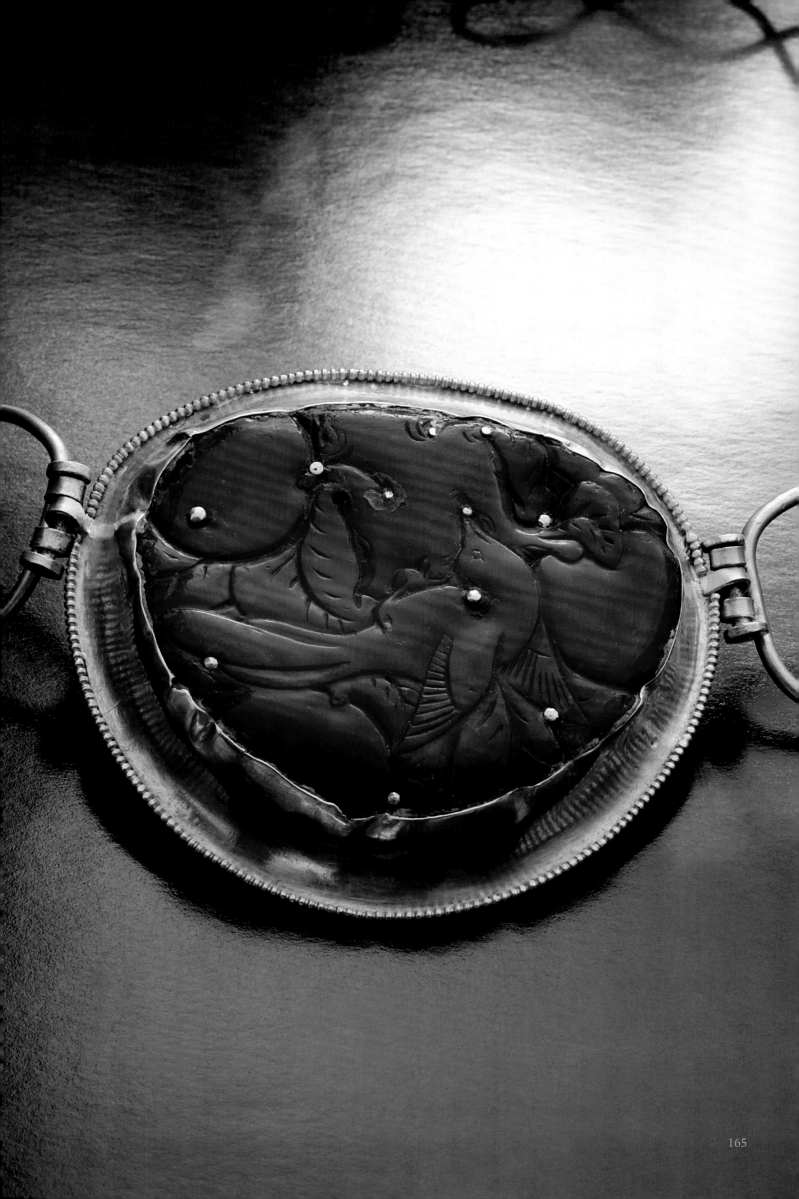

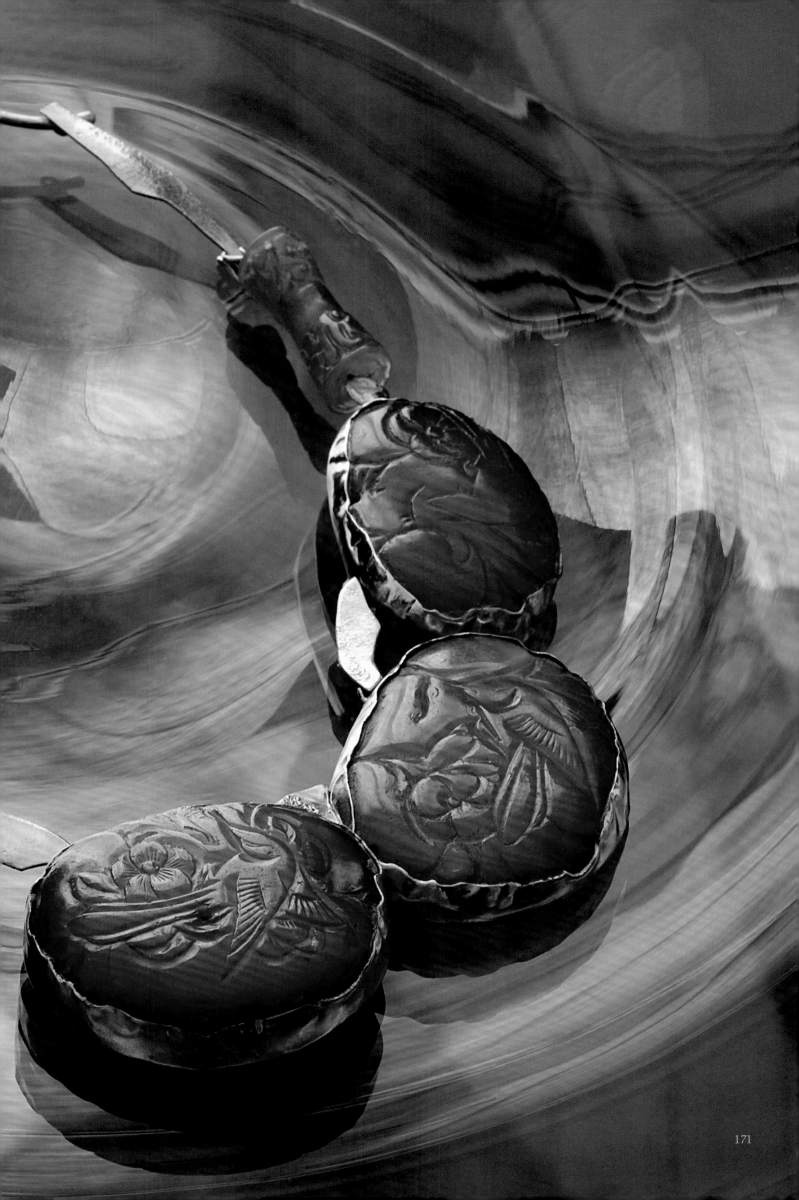

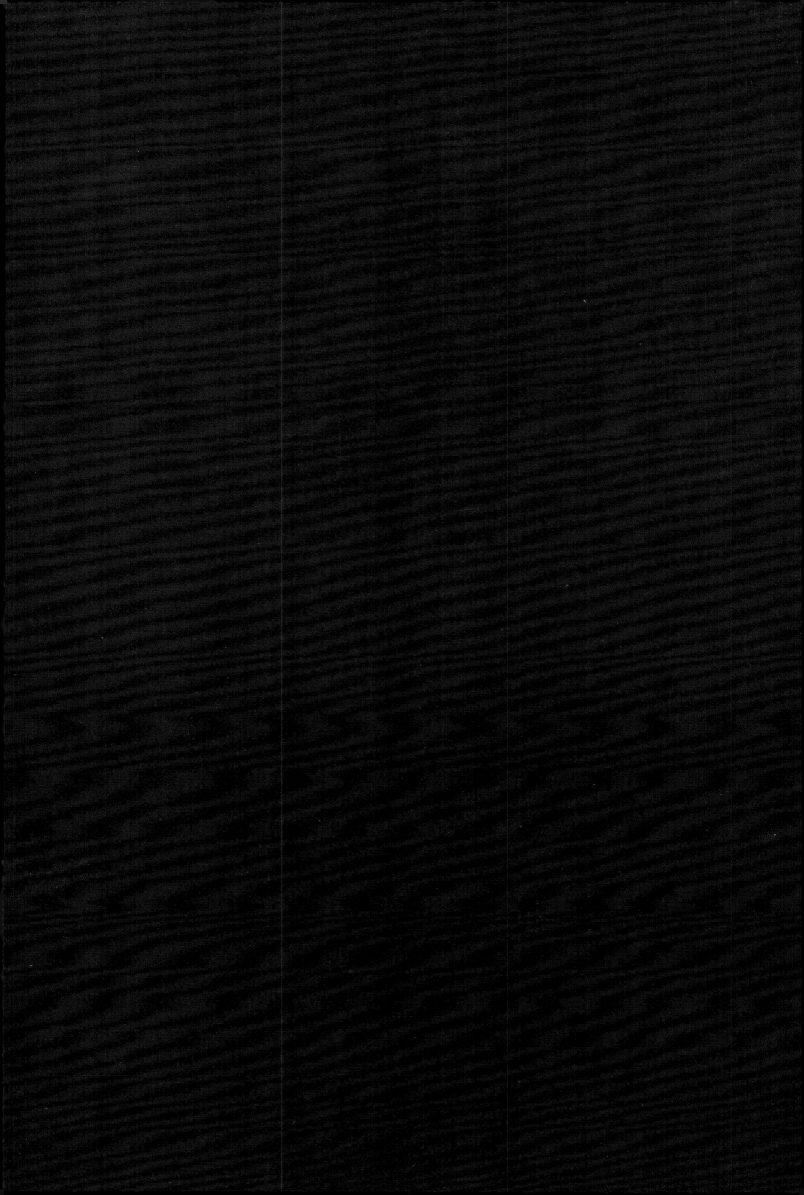

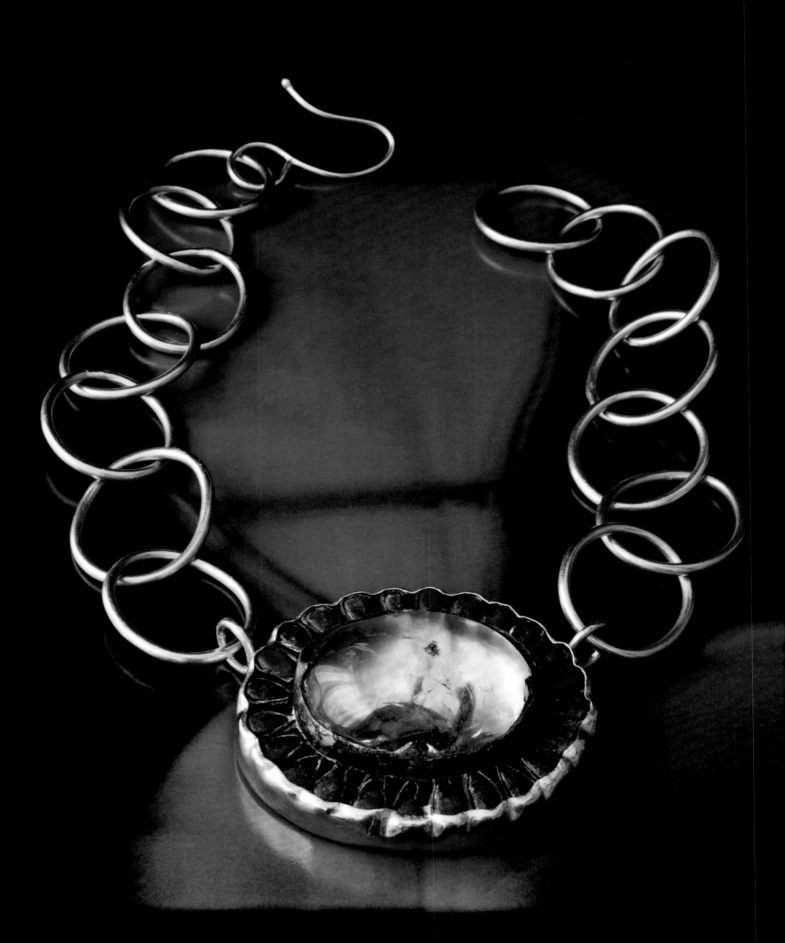

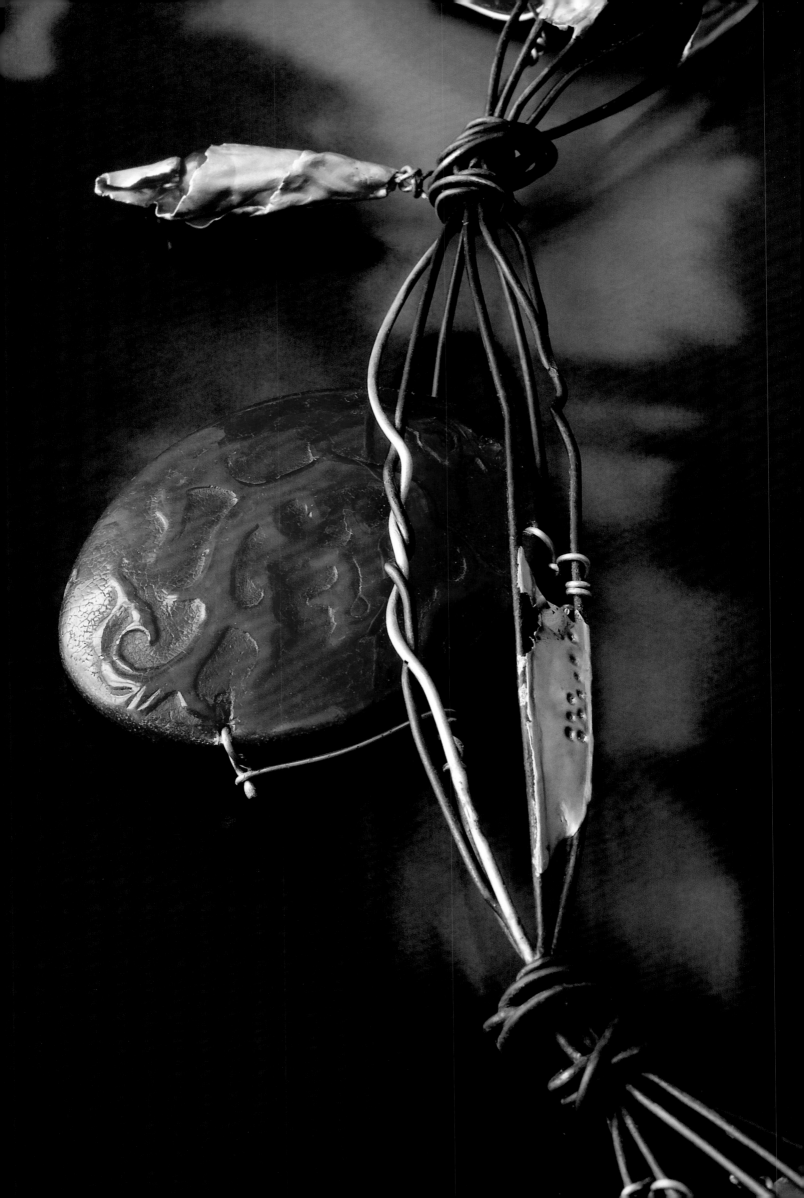

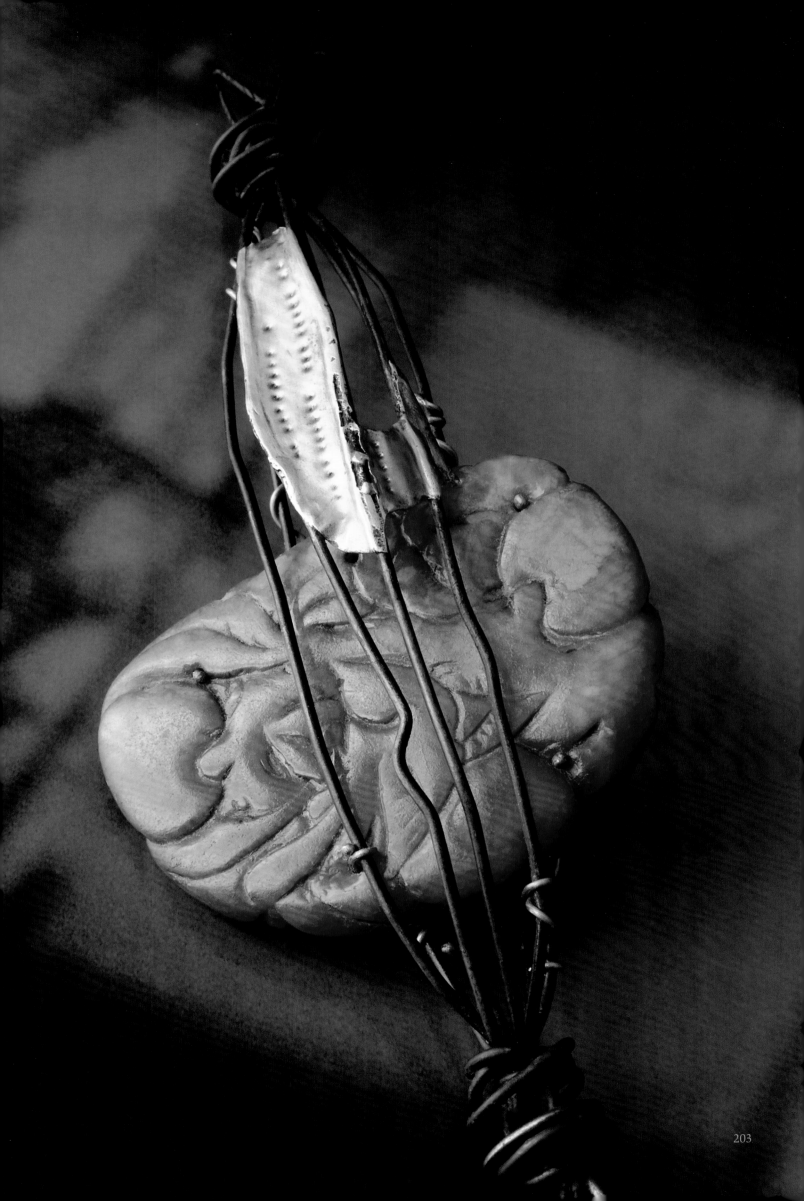

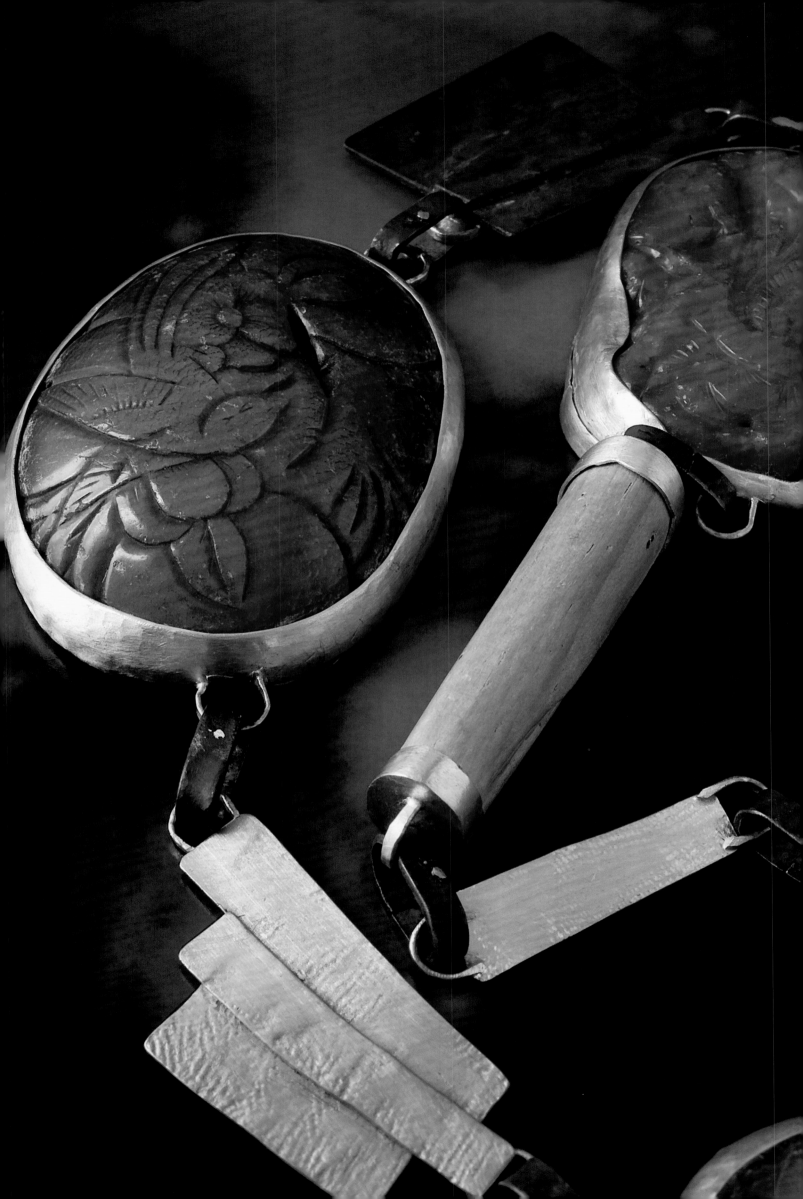

Ring
22 car. gold
Demantoid, Madagascar
4 × 4 cm (1⅝ × 1⅝ in.)
Ram Rijal
Page 17

Pendant
22 car. gold
Opals, Ethiopia
Emeralds
Diamonds
8 × 5 cm (3⅛ × 2 in.)
Ornella Iannuzzi
Page 23

Bracelet
22 car. gold
Black coral, Mexico
Semi-precious stones
5.6 × 7.5 cm (2¼ × 3 in.)
Ram Rijal
Pages 26–27

Bracelet
22 car. gold
Polyurethane
Semi-precious stones
5.5 × 8 cm (2⅛ × 3⅛ in.)
Gaetano Pesce
Ram Rijal
Page 30

Ring
22 car. gold
Polyurethane
Semi-precious stones
5 × 4.5 cm (2 × 1¾ in.)
Gaetano Pesce
Ram Rijal
Page 31

Necklace
22 car. gold
Chinese jade
56 × 26 cm (22 × 10¼ in.)
Ram Rijal
Page 35

Ring
22 car. gold
Opal, Ethiopia
3 × 3.5 cm (1⅛ × 1⅜ in.)
Ram Rijal
Page 36

Necklace
22 car. gold
Tourmaline
58 × 25 cm (22⅞ × 9⅞ in.)
Nan Nan Liu
Page 38

Necklace
22 car. gold
Baltic amber, Latvia
57 cm (22½ in.)
Ram Rijal
Page 45

Ring
22 car. gold
Demantoid, Madagascar
3.5 × 2.5 cm (1⅜ × 1 in.)
Ornella Iannuzzi
Page 49

Necklace
22 car. gold
Lapis, Afghanistan
60 × 38 cm (23⅝ × 15 in.)
Ram Rijal
Page 53

Cuff
22 car. gold
Black coral
8 × 7.8 cm (3⅛ × 3 in.)
Ram Rijal
Page 57

Necklace
22 car. gold
White Baltic amber, Estonia
76 cm (29⅞ in.)
Nan Nan Liu
Page 59

Ring
22 car. gold
4.5 × 2.5 cm (1¾ × 1 in.)
Ram Rijal
Page 64

Bracelet
22 car. gold
Coloured paper
6.5 × 7.5 cm (2½ × 3 in.)
Nan Nan Liu
Page 65

Necklace
22 car. gold
Ivory, 19th-century Dinka, Sudan
38 cm (15 in.)
Ram Rijal
Page 69

Necklace
22 car. gold
Crystal beads, India
48 cm (18⅞ in.)
Ram Rijal
Page 72

Torc
22 car. gold
Oxidized silver
Opals, Ethiopia
19 × 20 cm (7½ × 7⅞ in.)
Disa Allsopp
Page 74

Ring
22 car. gold
Oxidized silver
Opal, Ethiopia
4 × 2.5 cm (1⅝ × 1 in.)
Disa Allsopp
Page 79

Necklace
22 car. gold
Baltic amber, carved in China,
18th century
Rubies
Baroque pearls
54 cm (21¼ in.)
Daniel Azaro
Page 81

Bracelet
22 car. gold
Polyurethane
Lapis, Afghanistan
11 × 5.5 cm (4⅜ × 2⅛ in.)
Gaetano Pesce
Ram Rijal
Page 82

Ring
22 car. gold
Lapis, Afghanistan
4 × 3.5 cm (1⅝ × 1⅜ in.)
Ram Rijal
Page 87

Necklace
22 car. gold
Baroque pearls
Rubies
Emeralds
Sapphires
Diamonds
Demantoid
Peridot
Silver
113 cm (44½ in.)
Ram Rijal
Page 89

Necklace
22 car. gold
Baltic amber, carved in China,
18th century
Kingfisher feathers, China
Turquoise
55 cm (21⅝ in.)
Daniel Azaro
Page 90

Ring
22 car. gold
Amethyst
3.5 × 3.5 cm (1⅜ × 1⅜ in.)
Ram Rijal
Page 93

Brooch
22 car. gold
Black coral, Thailand
White coral, Thailand
Semi-precious stones
Cultured pearl
16.5 cm (6½ in.)
Ram Rijal
Page 96

Ring
22 car. gold
18 car. gold
2.5 × 2.5 cm (1 × 1 in.)
Nan Nan Liu
Page 100

Ring
22 car. gold
2.5 × 3 cm (1 × 1⅛ in.)
Ram Rijal
Page 101

Necklace
22 car. gold
Baltic amber, carved in China,
18th century
Black coral
Silk thread
28 cm (11 in.)
Daniel Azaro
Page 102

Ring
22 car. gold
Aquamarine
3 × 2 cm (1⅛ × ¾ in.)
Ram Rijal
Page 107

Necklace
22 car. gold
Tourmaline, Burma
25 × 15 cm (9⅞ × 5⅞ in.)
Ram Rijal
Page 109

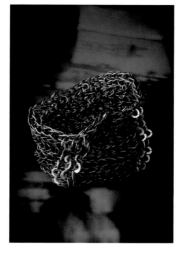

Bracelet
22 car. gold
Bronze
6 × 9.5 cm (2⅜ × 3¾ in.)
Syann van Niftrik
Page 113

Ring
22 car. gold vermeil
Baroque pearl
4.5 × 3 cm (1¾ × 1⅛ in.)
Ornella Iannuzzi
Page 115

Necklace
22 car. gold
Carnelian eye beads, Afghanistan
56 cm (22 in.)
Ram Rijal
Page 117

Ring
22 car. gold
Opal, Ethiopia
Black rhodium silver and
24 car. gold leaf
4.5 × 4.5 cm (1¾ × 1¾ in.)
Ornella Iannuzzi
Page 122

3 necklaces
22 car. gold
1st-century Roman glass beads,
Afghanistan
43, 59 and 61 cm
(16⅞, 23¼ and 24 in.)
Ram Rijal
Pages 126–127

Pendant
22 car. gold
Ivory ring, Dinka, Sudan
Chain: 68 cm (26¾ in.)
Ring: 6 × 6 cm (2⅜ × 2⅜ in.)
Ram Rijal
Page 129

Bracelet
22 car. gold
White coral, Thailand
Black coral, Mexico
Cultured pearls
5 × 7 cm (2 × 2¾ in.)
Ram Rijal
Page 133

Ring
22 car. gold
Black onyx
3.5 × 4 cm (1⅜ × 1⅝ in.)
Ram Rijal
Page 137

Necklace
22 car. gold
Baltic amber, carved in China,
18th century
White amber, Latvia
28 cm (11 in.)
Daniel Azaro
Page 138

Bracelet
22 car. gold
Aquamarine
7 × 6 cm (2¾ × 2⅜ in.)
Ram Rijal
Page 141

Necklace
22 car. gold
Amber
Coral
Aquamarine
Amethyst
Crystal
43 cm (16⅞ in.)
Ram Rijal
Page 143

Bracelet
22 car. gold
5 × 6 cm (2 × 2⅜ in.)
Ram Rijal
Page 144

Ring
22 car. gold
1.7 cm (⅝ in.)
Ram Rijal
Page 145

Ring
22 car. gold
Baroque pearl
3.8 × 3.5 cm (1½ × 1⅜ in.)
Ram Rijal
Page 147

Torc
22 car. gold
1st-century Roman glass beads,
Afghanistan
13 × 15 cm (5⅛ × 5⅞ in.)
Ram Rijal
Page 149

Necklace
22 car. gold
White amber, Lithuania
55 cm (21⅝ in.)
Ram Rijal
Page 151

Ring
22 car. gold
Bone, Cuba
4 × 4.5 cm (1⅝ × 1¾ in.)
Ram Rijal
Page 153

Pendant
22 car. gold
Emerald, Colombia
4.5 × 3.5 cm (1¾ × 1⅜ in.)
Ram Rijal
Page 154

Pendant
22 car. gold
Emerald, Colombia
Chain: 24 car. gold
Emerald: 4 × 2.5 cm (1⅝ × 1 in.)
Ram Rijal
Page 155

Necklace
22 car. gold
Coral, Morocco, 19th century
53 cm (20⅞ in.)
Ram Rijal
Page 157

Bracelet
22 car. gold
Ivory button, Namibia, 19th century
60 × 85 cm (23⅝ × 33½ in.)
Ram Rijal
Page 159

Belt buckle
22 car. gold
Aquamarine
Sapphires
Diamonds
10 × 7.5 cm (3⅞ × 3 in.)
Ram Rijal
Page 163

Torc
22 car. gold
Baltic amber, carved in China,
18th century
23 cm (9 in.)
Daniel Azaro
Page 164

Ring
22 car. gold
White coral, Thailand
Semi-precious stones
4 × 4 cm (1⅝ × 1⅝ in.)
Ram Rijal
Page 166

Pendant
22 car. gold
White coral, Thailand
Semi-precious stones
7 × 3.5 cm (2¾ × 1⅜ in.)
Ram Rijal
Page 167

Ring
22 car. gold
Uncut ruby
3 × 2.5 cm (1⅛ × 1 in.)
Ram Rijal
Page 169

Necklace
22 car. gold
Baltic amber, carved in China,
18th century
Jade
19 cm (7½ in.)
Daniel Azaro
Page 173

Ring
22 car. gold
Opal, Ethiopia
3.5 × 3.5 cm (1⅜ × 1⅜ in.)
Ram Rijal
Page 174

Ring
22 car. gold
Opal
3.5 × 2.5 cm (1⅜ × 1 in.)
Ram Rijal
Page 175

Pendant
22 car. gold
White coral, Thailand
Pearl
7 × 6.5 cm (2¾ × 2½ in.)
Ram Rijal
Page 177

Rings
22 car. gold
Emerald
3 × 2.5 cm (1⅛ × 1 in.),
2.5 × 2 cm (1 × ¾ in.)
Ram Rijal
Page 178

Torc
22 car. gold
Baltic amber, carved in China,
18th century
White amber, Lithuania
14 × 16 cm (5½ × 6¼ in.)
Ram Rijal
Page 181

Pendant
22 car. gold
Coral
11 × 10 cm (4⅜ × 3⅞ in.)
(26 cm/10¼ in. incl. torc)
Ram Rijal
Page 183

Ring
22 car. gold
Opal, Ethiopia
4 × 4.5 cm (1⅝ × 1¾ in.)
Ram Rijal
Page 184

Pendant
22 car. gold
White coral, Burma
Semi-precious stones
7 × 8.5 cm (2¾ × 3⅜ in.)
Ram Rijal
Page 187

Pendant
22 car. gold
Demantoid, Madagascar
Diamond
10 × 5 cm (3⅞ × 2 in.)
Ornella Iannuzzi
Page 189

Ring
22 car. gold
Black tourmaline
3 × 2.5 cm (1⅛ × 1 in.)
Ram Rijal
Page 193

Necklace
22 car. gold
Crystal and lapis pendant, Tibet,
18th century
6 × 7 cm (2⅜ × 2¾ in.)
Ram Rijal
Page 194

Ring
22 car. gold
Ivory, Dinka, Sudan
4 × 3 cm (1⅝ × 1⅛ in.)
Ram Rijal
Page 197

Necklace
22 car. gold
Tourmaline
Rubies
Sapphires
Emeralds
50 cm (19⅝ in.)
Ram Rijal
Page 198

Necklace
22 car. gold
Baltic amber, carved in China,
18th century
Iron, leather and string
27 cm (10⅝ in.)
Ram Rijal
Page 201

Necklace
22 car. gold
Black coral
Crystal
Aquamarines
24 × 17 cm (9½ × 6¾ in.)
Ram Rijal
Page 205

Ring
22 car. gold
Emerald
4 × 3.5 cm (1⅝ × 1⅜ in.)
Ram Rijal
Page 207

Necklace
22 car. gold
Ivory roundels, Dinka,
Sudan
63.7 cm (25 in.)
Ram Rijal
Page 208

Necklace
22 car. gold
Baltic amber, carved in
China, 18th century
48 cm (18⅞ in.)
Ram Rijal
Page 209

Ring
22 car. gold
Opal, Ethiopia
4 × 3 cm (1⅝ × 1⅛ in.)
Ram Rijal
Page 211

Necklace
22 car. gold
Pearls
Diamond
42 cm (16½ in.)
Ram Rijal
Page 213

Necklace
22 car. gold
Baltic amber, carved in China,
18th century
Driftwood and iron
58 cm (22⅞ in.)
Helga Mogensen
Page 215

Pendant
22 car. gold
Amethyst
7 × 9 cm (2¾ × 3½ in.)
Ram Rijal
Page 216

Ring
22 car. gold
Uncut ruby
3 × 2 cm (1⅛ × ¾ in.)
Ram Rijal
Page 217

Necklace
22 car. gold
Baltic amber, carved in China,
18th century
Jade, Burma
48 cm (18⅞ in.)
Ram Rijal
Page 219

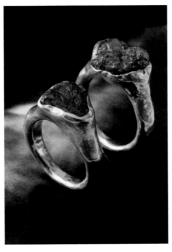

Rings
22 car. gold
Black diamond
2.5 × 0.8 cm (1 × ¼ in.),
3 × 0.9 cm (1⅛ × ⅜ in.)
Ram Rijal
Page 221

Ring
22 car. gold
Ivory, Dinka, Sudan
Semi-precious stones
3.5 × 3.5 cm (1⅜ × 1⅜ in.)
Ram Rijal
Page 222

Ring
22 car. gold
Bone, Cuba
Pearls
Semi-precious stones
3.5 × 4.5 cm (1⅜ × 1¾ in.)
Ram Rijal
Page 223

Ornella Iannuzzi is an award-winning French jeweler. 'My work is a celebration of the amazing beauty created by the earth's activity over millions of years,' she says. 'I question many preconceptions about jewelry design. I approach my jewelry in a similar way to small sculpture. This is a medium through which I challenge perceptions of preciousness. There is always an artistic concept behind every piece of jewelry I make.'

Ram Rijal was born in Nepal, and in his youth would watch the craftsmen of Kathmandu as they hammered and forged. On his arrival in London in the late 1980s, he put those memories into use as a self-taught jeweler. His 22 carat hammered-gold creations are inspired by the very stones he chooses to work with: not by their clarity or purity, or their value as a commodity, but by what radiates from them. He also conceives and executes the perfect setting for stones that are brought to him as commissions. Ram enjoys a faithful following of sophisticated international collectors, and has created unique pieces for the finest galleries and London department stores. His work has been featured in publications such as *Vogue*, *Tatler* and the *Financial Times*.

Disa Allsopp graduated from Edinburgh College of Art. She has exhibited in solo and group shows in the UK, Barbados, the USA and Italy. Her work has appeared in the Victoria & Albert Museum, Sotheby's Contemporary Decorative Arts Show, Goldsmiths' Fair, Origin Fair and the New York Gift Fair, to name but a few. She works in London.

Syann van Niftrik was born in South Africa and originally trained as a ceramic designer. She says: 'I work in gold, silver and bronze, and it is the materials and the process that I enjoy; and I like these to be evident in the finished piece. The comfort of the wearer is paramount, so in making jewelry I look at the way in which a piece moves and interacts with the body. I enjoy drama, but the bond that a person develops in the wearing of a piece is what I strive for.'

Nan Nan Liu initially studied accountancy in China before training for eight years in jewelry design and silversmithing. She now enjoys her creative life in London. Her work reflects experimentation and a balance between nature and ornamentation. After looking at the circular rings within a tree and the beauty crafted by nature over time, she started making a collection of layered paper and fine metal jewelry. Using a painstaking technique that involves applying hand-formed layers of gold or silver, one by one, to each of her pieces, she creates unique forms that capture the essence of the arboreal phenomenon.

Helga Mogensen is an Icelandic jeweler working in the heart of Reykjavik. 'I am a member of a creative co-op of eleven women and we have a craft shop through which we sell our pieces, be it ceramics, clothing or jewelry,' she states. 'It's been wonderful to be a part of this collective. I also take part in foreign and group shows such as "From the Coolest Corner", a touring exhibition of Nordic jewelry. I often go to the north of Iceland to collect the driftwood for my pieces.'

Daniel Azaro was born in Buenos Aires, where he studied architecture, but settled in London in the 1970s. During his travels he moved away from working at a large scale, and instead began to design and make objects that were wearable and comfortable. He appreciates all materials, and his selection is based on their intrinsic rather than commercial value. Whether natural or manmade, ancient or new, found or industrial, precious or worthless, in Azaro's hands they are transformed from their original state into stunning new creations.

Narisa Chakrabongse was brought up in Cornwall and Bangkok. She has a BA (Hons.) in Art History from the Courtauld Institute, University of London, and an MA in Southeast Asian Area Studies from the School of Oriental and African Studies, University of London. In 1992 she founded River Books, a publishing company specializing in books on the art, history and culture of mainland Southeast Asia. Since then, she has edited and published more than 100 titles. In 1998, she opened a small boutique hotel in the grounds of her Bangkok home, Chakrabongse Villas, where she lives with her husband Gee and two sons, Hugo and Dominic. She has known Mimi for twenty-five years, is a big fan of her work and is saving to buy a piece of her jewelry.

Noelle Hoeppe's photographs have been published in magazines, advertising campaigns and books. Clients include *AD France*, Cartier, Dosa, Hermès, Ladurée, Laurent-Perrier, Puiforcat and Taittinger. Her personal work has been shown in solo exhibitions in Paris and New York, and has been featured in group exhibitions internationally. Her work is included in public and private collections in France and abroad. She lives and works in Paris.

Malgosia Szemberg was art director at the Condé Nast magazine *World of Interiors* for ten years, and has collaborated with artists and designers in Europe, the USA and Latin America as creative director, curator and consultant. Her visual storytelling mixes rigour with opulent fancy in the design of artists' monographs and avant-garde books with innovative handmade details. She has worked on books such as *Edible Schoolyard: A Universal Idea* and *40 years of Chez Panisse: The Power of Gathering*, both by Alice Waters, and a monograph on the London-based Chilean sculptor Fernando Casasempere, with whom she is preparing new book projects. She lives and works in London.

Mimi Lipton was born in Austria, and educated in Belgium and England. She worked at the Institute of Contemporary Arts in London, where she was able to further her interest in modern art. She has been a lifelong collector and patron in all things Tibetan, and has travelled extensively in Africa and Asia. Publications include *The Tiger Rugs of Tibet*, *Stacking Wood* with Thorsten Düser, *In the Oriental Style: A Sourcebook of Decoration and Design* with Michael Freeman and Siân Evans, and *Gold Jewelry from Tibet and Nepal* with Jane Singer. She was also closely involved in the research and realization of the exhibition 'Peoples of the Golden Triangle' and the accompanying book by Paul and Elaine Lewis.

ACKNOWLEDGMENTS

This book would never have happened without the insistence of my indulgent partner and friends, who were convinced that my late-in-life efforts would be of interest to others. Thank you all for your faith and support and meddling suggestions. Special thanks to the talented, creative international jewelers I encountered over many years. I loved working with you all and am grateful for your unfailing enthusiasm. You are all stars. Thank you Nan Nan, Helga, Disa, Ornella, Syann, Ram and Daniel. You have enhanced my life.

Invaluable creative input came from Malgosia Szemberg, who directed the photography and designed the book. Her empathy with my jewelry is very much apparent.

Noelle, you succeeded in creating a visual feast in the portrayal of my jewelry. Your photos are breathtaking, chapeau chapeau.

Thank you Narisa for your introduction. You captured in a few lines and thoughts the essence of this book.

I must applaud Thomas Neurath for his vision and the title of this book (Thomas, what were you thinking of?). Finally, many thanks to the Thames & Hudson team.

Mimi Lipton